Player Piano

Player Piano

poems

Conrad Hilberry

Louisiana State University Press

Baton Rouge

1999

Manufactured in the United States of America
First printing
08 07 06 05 04 03 02 01 00 99
5 4 3 2 1

Designer: Amanda McDonald Scallan
Typeface: Sabon
Typesetter: Coghill Composition Co., Inc.
Printer and binder: Thomson-Shore, Inc.

Library of Congress Cataloging-in-Publication Data

Hilberry, Conrad.
    Player piano : poems / Conrad Hilberry.
        p. cm.
    ISBN 0-8071-2379-X (cloth : alk. paper). — ISBN 0-8071-2380-3
    (pbk. : alk. paper)
    PS3558.I384P58   1999
    811'.54—dc21   99-28003
                                                           CIP

The author gratefully acknowledges the editors of the following journals, in which many of
the poems herein first appeared, sometimes in different forms: *Encore,* "Otavalo"; *Gettys-
burg Review,* "The Calvinist," "The Expatriates," "Falling in Love," "Figures in an Improb-
able Landscape," "Macabre," "Mexico: Waiting for the Gas," "Shepherd," "The Slurry";
Kenyon Review, "The Good Grief," "Heraclitus on Fire," "On the Promontory"; *Poetry
Northwest,* "Mstislav Rostropovich," "The Spit"; *Shenandoah,* "Avenida Montejo," "The
Eye," "Income Tax," "Martha Dancing," "Player Piano," "Responsibility," "Tepoztlán,"
"Touch"; *Snowy Egret,* "Lullaby," "Night Song"; *Tamaqua,* "Descartes: A Lecture at the
Sea," "Father Alfaro," "Love Poem with Scenery," "Meeting, at a Party, a Woman with an
Artificial Larynx"; *Third Coast, "Qui Tollis Peccata Mundi"; Virginia Quarterly Review,*
"Night Sky with Tree," "Omens."

"An Anniversary" first appeared in *My Poor Elephant* (Longstreet Press, 1962), edited by
Eve Shelnutt.

The author offers special thanks to the Virginia Center for the Creative Arts, where a num-
ber of these poems were drafted, and to Dabney Stuart, Diane Seuss-Brakeman, Larry Bar-
rett, and Ed and Brownie Galligan for their extraordinarily generous and insightful help.

For my family
and for all my students over the years

Contents

T h r e e

The Expatriates

Here in the sun, the long December days
defy sadness. Courtyards, narrow streets,
walls still warm at evening. And flowers—
geraniums, conchas, the bleeding fuchsias—
each with its own faint smell, incense settling
on the cobblestones. The bent arms
of bougainvillaea are tricked out in crimson
or magenta. In the north, we remember,
our grief had reasons: confinement and cold,
the pipes frozen, new snow so deep you wake,
look out, and sink back into the week-long
loneliness. But here on this high plateau,
the air is thin, the clouds thin, the days
attenuated, beaten like gold until
they stretch unbroken from horizon to
horizon. At long distance we hear the voices
of our children. "Really," we say, "how are you?"
"Oh, thanks, I'm all right," a sadness,
traveling two thousand miles over
desert and dry riverbed, thinning down
to a single fiber—as in the garden
the orchids lay their small mouths on the neck
of the evening, as grackles scream into the pruned
trees, as lemon tea steeps in the pot
on the wrought-iron table and we talk
of conveniences and inconveniences.
Far away, a dog howls as though
the enchilada woman splashed his eyes
with hot grease. A taxicab backs up
a one-way street, saving gas. The plastered
walls, the cobblestones, still warm us. Boys
kick a soccer ball. A woman carries
a car battery on her head. We see
all this as though we were remembering it,
as though the day had stretched on into March

and we were looking back through months
of transparent air. Above the tower
of San Isidro, a weightless scrap of moon
drifts on the sunset like a shallow boat.

Tepoztlán

On the Day of the Dead, when
midnight comes, the people here
ring all the bells in town
so the dead can find their way
back home. Some say
it works: they come. I imagine
one of them, a child,
hearing the bells like voices
across water, like a small
wind stepping from island
to island, touching the palms
and mangroves, waking a dog
curled under the boards
of a dock. She moves
as the bells call her,
to her own town, her house,
but hesitates outside a window.
She sees her younger sisters,
women now and married, grown
sad it seems, or harsh,
or tired. If they saw her
how could they know her?
Who would comfort whom?
She pauses at the curtain,
then comes in, smells
the fruits and spices
they have set out, touches
her doll, her dress, hears
their voices, unmistakable
even now. She feels
crowded by their large
arms, their hair, the smell
of garlic and cilantro left
from supper. This is what it is
to love, she remembers—

teeth, breasts, talk heavy
with obligation. She sits
with them at the table
as they dip empanadas
in the red sauce,
three young women and an old one,
hungry, worried, holding
each other's shoulders,
laughing, describing Juan Diego
and how he went about to cure
his sick horse. The girl
moves back to the window
and eases the twist of air
which is herself
into the small wind
and the thin clatter
of bells. She remembers
a visit once to the north
in deep winter. When
she and her mother walked
in the snow, it cried
under their feet. The cold
grabbed her in both arms
and squeezed until she could
hardly breathe. She was afraid
of this terrible affection.
What did it ask of her?
How could she ever return it?

Avenida Montejo

The letter slips through
the slot: he's been to Mérida
again, the pyramids,

the jungle. She remembers
their hotel on the Avenida
Montejo, talking away

the humid nights
in the restaurant where
the Mayan piano player

knew all the old show tunes.
She reads again—the foreign
stamp and thin paper,

the awkward, angled writing,
the words settled there
where they can never

rise or turn. She kisses
the envelope and leans
back, completely in love

for once, tilting her head
as though she stood in
the shower, as though

the hot stream were running
through her hair and down
her shoulders, as though nothing

could ever complicate
the thin fingers of water.

Night Sky with Tree

She cuts away the moon, lifts out
the stars. Holding the knife precisely

in her fist, she carves away
the branches of the sassafras,

hollowing the fragrant, mittened
leaves. She inks the block and prints:

an empty sky, patterned
by curving absences, the lovely

insubstantial syllables
of *moon* and *stars* and *sassafras*.

The Good Grief

Three of us are quoting Father
Hopkins over breakfast, *fresh thoughts
care for, can you?* the poet breaking
syntax over his knee, dry sticks

for the fire. *What heart heard of,
ghost guessed.* Young grief and old
from the old griever. We walk out
into the fall morning and there's

the third-quarter moon almost down
to the trees, barely visible
in the sunlight, a pale basket
picking up the leavings. We three,

who think we know what branch
the grief-leaves grow on,
look to the Blue Ridge just bleeding
into red—the summer, the moon,

ourselves, all waning. This is
the good grief, sadness ripe
as the smell of wild pears by the road.
But you, Margaret, wake at five,

shaking, empty, digging your thin
fingers into the rock, sheer
cliffs of fall, and hang on,
praying for day to come.

Next week the moon will shrink
to nothing, sky black, the valley
crossed only by the Norfolk & Southern
dragging its endless freight.

After sunset, over the rise
in the west, a new moon—
anguish scratched on the sky,
a stroke too thin to hide

anything. Your moon. Absolute.
Still, each night it eases higher
in the dark, less empty.
Someday it may blur to this pale coin

we finger in the morning air.

Qui Tollis Peccata Mundi

Ordinarily, the rocks pitch down
when they break loose from the chimneys
up on the cliff—pitch down,
smash whatever they come to,
and hiss on into the sea. But this huge
boulder, *peccatum mundi,* rolled slowly,
bouncing on the talus then lumbering into
the forest. We heard it coming. It flattened
pines, lurched through the riverbed
then down here into the heat, shouldered
palms and banana trees like some elephant
with a long memory. It settled on our house,
pushed in the roof. We couldn't stand up.
Had to crawl in, sleep with that boulder
on our chests. We knew it was somebody's
fault. The children grew up under it,
thought houses must be like that. Then
somehow You did it. Lifted it. Took
it away. *Christe. Domine.* We stood again,
breathed, looked out at the sea-swells
carrying blessings our way, bowing
toward us, offering at our feet the rich
foam. *Tollis* is the word, all right.
Restless under the rock, we heard
the air wince as though a bell swung
high overhead, paused with its mouth
wide open, upward, then fell and struck.
It tolled and tolled, its pitch almost
too high for us to hear, or too low,
but we could feel it wrench our flesh—
and, in the rock, crevices opened. Bong.
Bong. And the rock split, crumbled,
fell away. A monkey lifted
a white bromeliad from a branch
and sucked the sweet fruit at its heart.

A parrot shouted. We raised the children
above our heads and danced.

We have restored the roof of our house
and we fish again in the open sea.
Morning fog congeals and runs like mercy
down our arms. Occasionally, clearing
a few yards for squash or beans, we curse
the hacked tangle of roots, the blackflies,
curse the heat and our lives, curse
the rutting peccaries that raid our plot.
Only occasionally they come, the peccaries
with their black hair and white lips—
the smoky pork taste of their flesh.

Mexico: Waiting for the Gas

At first, it's urgent—pressure down to zero.
Call the Gas. Water goes cold, the stove
flares and flickers out. Call again
each day, and each day the Gas is promised. *Hoy,*
claro. I stay at home. If the Gas should come
while I was out, who could imagine it coming
a second time? The madness of waiting
for a simple thing—hot soup, a shower.
Somewhere the Gas, huge as a cement truck,
lumbers through narrow streets. When it turns
a corner, a boy hops off and props a sign
on the cobblestones: *No Pasar. El Gas.*
Enormous elephant in the Tuesday market—
no one can predict where it will lurch
or stop. Like money. Like the police.
Like typhoid fever. These white rooms become
a hospital abandoned by the staff.
Let the foreigner cure himself. Cold,
shaking in the bare room, wondering
how long this emptiness has been coming on.

The seventh day, I climb to the roof to see
a palm against low-flying clouds, the green
of Juarez Park, basketball courts, dry hills.
The Gas will rumble up from that direction,
from the south, the largest moving thing
in town. The scissor sharpener blows his eerie
five-note whistle. In a clay pot nearby,
a fuchsia hangs its lavish globs of color.
Waiting becomes easy, as when an IV
drips into a vein. Dreaming,
I see the driver climb from the cab, call
to his partner on the roof to toss the rope down,
hoist the nozzle, and let it flow.

Now the light has shifted, catching the fuchsia's
bleeding shapes against the whitewashed wall.
Texture and shadow—as in a darkroom years ago,
I waited, felt the vague grays come up
under my fingers till suddenly the features
became themselves, the likeness unmistakable
but strange, not myself at all. Waiting,
coaxing a face from the developer,
eyes gone, hollow cheeks drawn back
around the teeth. The mummies
of Guanajuato writhe not far from here.
I suppose they, too, could be said to wait.

Macabre

In the old woodcuts, the leering
skeletons approach and tap us
on the shoulder, cutting in,

requesting the next dance.
The civility of it, the formality—
we dance a few turns to the fluty

music, fingers hooked in rib bones,
then slip off two by two
into the bushes. Getting born

is violent—flesh tearing
and crying out. But dying is
honor your partner

and do-si-do. How nimble
all the moves.
How trim the shrubbery.

O t a v a l o

At the edge of the great market,
in a booth with woven bowls

and hangings, two women sit,
cheerful, dressed in black.

While they talk, they reach
in a plastic bag

for live beetles,
pull off their wings, casually

as though they might be shelling
peas or knitting,

and toss the still-live
bodies in a jar

where they seethe
and burrow. Sold and fried,

they become a snack
on market day, *corpus*

crispy, and the wings will be layered
like delicate scales

on fans or scarves or headgear,
taking to the air again.

Figures in an Improbable Landscape

Arresting, those eerie Chinese mountains,
incredibly steep, floating up out of the mist,
the long white line of a waterfall, some twisted

trees in precise detail, and at the lower right
a figure, almost invisible, driving
a cluster of mules. Is there such a place?

Where was Fan K'uan standing when he painted it?
Did he make it up, as he says, "from my own heart"
or steal it from Li Ch'eng, his master?

Today, Fan K'uan, I'm walking that gray thread
at the bottom of your scroll. Here at Cusín,
near Otavalo, the road curves below

a steep field, each row of corn on its own
narrow terrace, looking at the roots
of the row above it, desperate agriculture,

as though each generation had to hang on
and ripen a few seeds to drop to the row
below. A voice seems to fall from the sky,

and there at the top of the field, immensely
high, a girl waves and calls. From somewhere
on the road ahead, another girl calls back—

thin voices in the thin air, a few syllables
each way, deep in this gash in the Andes.
Now a herd approaches, moving toward town—

a dozen sheep, four cows, two pigs, and a bare-
foot woman with a huge bundle on her back,
covered with a plastic sheet. They move

slowly. The animals pull at the grass
along the road, and the woman limps after them,
swinging a small whip. The pigs snort

and slosh up out of the gulley. As they pass,
I call hello to the woman, and, yes, she turns—
but her face is deranged, eyes askew, mouth

twisted to a line and a hole now that she
tries to speak. Her voice falls out
in a garble of sound, hoarse, a greeting

or curse. She limps a step or two and cracks
a cow's rump with the whip. It lurches
in a cow-gallop then settles back to a walk.

What do you think, Fan K'uan?
Could she be the figure driving
your mules? Is she anyone we know?

The Eye

I

Picture a cobblestone street,
doors, three flycatchers
on a dead cypress, a woman—

crosslegged on a blanket—
peeling the red cactus fruit.
Clouds, electric wires, four

lean dogs. To live
by the eye alone, to flatten
the world to shadings, planes,

depths in space but not in time,
none of the past seeping in
with its brags and humiliations.

II

In an instant the eye takes in
shapes and spaces, colors, corners,
faces, oddities of light. But words
walk one behind the other,

barefoot penitents setting out
at night, carrying
the old shrine on their shoulders.
Sometimes they sing on the long trek,

finding their footing, shifting
the weight. There's little here
for the eye. Dawn holds off
till they've outwalked the dark.

III

A flash on the retina, when it's
translated into words, becomes
stained glass with Lazarus leaded in,
trying to rise from the dead.

IV

On a narrow street, at dusk,
children run and hide
in doorways, behind barrels,
around the crumbling corner
of a house—half a face

beyond the fender of a car,
a boy crouched behind
a low stone wall.
Across the street, a woman
with a lined face leans

on a doorframe, expressionless,
one arm over her head.
The girl who's It
runs, stops, looks,
and calls a name.

From all corners of the dark
children come out, chanting
e-qui-vo-ca-ci-ón, e-qui-vo-ca-ci-ón.
They mean she's got it wrong,
called the wrong name,

but the word hangs in the air.
She counts, they run again,
and the street is empty
except for a woman's face
against the wall.

V

The eye, that cool looker, comes back
to her face, the doorframe, the faint
shadow cast by the streetlight—the dark

beside her on the stones. Shapes, too,
have etymologies. The lean face
must have been here when words were
a single syllable. Indigenous.
But indigenous to what? To this bare
country? To the wall? To the eye's own
sadness? Certain slopes and textures
twine around the optic nerve like smells
from childhood or the touch of hair
or steel. Lips and tongue have always
known their weakness. And now the eye
comes back to that face—and to a boy's
elbow, the white of his shirt, his cheek
in hiding curved against the dark.
The eye, the eye, too, falls in love.

T_{wo}

Player Piano

She was right: basement was the place for it.
Who wants a Pianola in the dining room?
It's not an instrument, not a household
object even, more a curiosity.

So with a rented dolly and four big friends
from work, he eased it down the cellar stairs,
across the concrete to its place against
the wall. Now he leans back on the bench

and pumps the Basement Rag. His youngest daughter
sits beside him on the bench within
the light of the gooseneck lamp, the dog curls
on the rug, and always the ghostly fingers move,

the left hand striding and the right hand climbing
down out of the high notes. Four of them,
father, daughter, dog, and piano player,
all in a circle of light, the roll unwinding

its dots and dashes, music clattering out,
and no one saying anything. "Hey,
Cosby's on," his wife calls down the stairs.
"Why not come on up?" And so they sit

in the kitchen, laughing at Rudy and the Cos.
Afterwards, homework and bed—and he drifts
back to the basement, back to the wooden music.
Gradually, his wife becomes sarcastic,

as if he were counterfeiting bills down there,
or dissecting cats. His daughter says she isn't
coming down. But he believes the piano
brings him closer to them all. It's something

he can count on, almost like a law
of nature, not needing praise or inspiration,
sticking to its version of the story.
The roll scrolling in front of him is

Morse code talking to people in other basements
or in huts or lean-to's—Sarasota, Caracas,
up-country Liberia. The key taps out
news of high winds, the river rising, families

sheltered in the local school, news
of people he's never met, clicking in a voice
without inflection, neither speech
nor silence. The longs and shorts, the steady

white keys and the black must carry
through the studs of the house, he thinks,
easing the children into sleep.
He hears a pipe muttering

and knows his wife is drawing water for
a bath. It stops. She must be in the tub.
He taps a message on the pipe, binary,
the way nerves talk, signaling across

the gaps, need and love condensed to dots
and dashes. She must hear it as she steams
and lathers in the bath, metallic music
played by no one's fingers on the pipes.

Falling in Love

From the time I could hold
the crayon, I did more
than scribble. I drew
circles with four

sticks coming out—two arms,
two legs—and moved on
to figures with pants and elbows,
faces long as my own.

Then to the luscious finger-
paints. Now here I am
doing acrylics and cracked
batiks all of the same

subject—myself—the eyes
blue-green and innocent,
the nose, the offhand
gesture of the lips bent

almost to a smile where
the brush touches delicately.
I have the latest face
silk-screened on the T-

shirt I wear under
the Oxford cloth, next to my
skin. At the party, you
and I meet, talk casually,

exchange stories. Button
by button, I undo
my shirt, you undo your
sweater until the two

pictures peer out at each
other, glance hesitantly—
eyebrows, cheekbones, teeth.
Liking what they see,

they unbutton all the way,
look into each other's eyes,
come closer until the faces
meet and kiss.

Income Tax

In March, I see numbers in the trees,
twigs twisted into 9's and 2's, a sky
full of numbers. Shouldn't they add up,

in a few weeks, to a green sum? I sort
through checks and scraps of paper: air fare, books
and journals, contributions, losses, moving

the totals from Schedule A to line 34,
rounding the numbers to eliminate
the ragged edge along the right-hand margin.

Gradually the year is justified.
The indecisions and remorse, the days
and weeks tangled in words—all that

has disappeared. I watch the numbers arch
and meet, line 50 (bartering transactions)
just matching line 8c. Amazingly,

we owe only a little more than we
have paid already. I step back. There
on the table stands my handmade Taj Mahal—

the symmetry, the fine stone ornament
of interlocking numbers. Sealing it,
I walk to the box and drop the envelope in.

The flap clangs. Through a light fog, I see
the maple on the corner, trunk muscling up
as though it knows where it's going, then

dividing, the huge limbs crossing and elbowing
as they reach toward the filigree at the edge.
Now the real year rushes back, everything

half-spoken, hurtful, longing to come whole.
A faint sun opens out of the fog, and the maple
frays, as though each bud had hatched

an insect stretching its green-gold wings.

The Calvinist

I like to think words go
their own way—like *waterspout*
or *sleep* or *Aztec soup*—but
in the chamber just behind

my tongue a Calvinist
sits at a thin-legged desk,
interjecting, editing. He
adds his touch, wrapping

a small message around the leg
of each pigeon as it comes
from the dovecote. The words
fly out, clattering white

against the sky, circling,
flashing in the sun like bits
of torn paper. But then
they feel the compass-pull,

feel the slight weight
of the message on their legs
and in a ragged line
head for home.

Mstislav Rostropovich

Row J, Top Balcony, Hill Auditorium, Ann Arbor

Far below us, the curved walls converge
to a tiny circle of light. In it, a bald
man sits, holding a cello between his knees
as a father might hold a child.

He bows the strings simply, telling a story
we all have heard before. We did not know
each other, but everyone on the steep bank
leans together to follow

the words, the working out of the old plot.
It is as we remember it, but clearer,
everything told just as it must have happened—
the knocking on the door,

the gift of a shirt, the flowers, the dark road.
He catches the lift or falter of each voice
and lets a simile unfold like wood
smoke. The action goes

as we know it must, tangled in jealously, the bird
lost, the lovers misunderstanding. The story
pauses and plummets like water over a rock.
Silence. The cellist reaches for

a handful of high notes—ourselves in the top
balcony. He finds us right where he left us
and plays us pure and sweet as a bunch of onions
hanging from the rafters.

Martha Dancing

Martha wants to dance. When she was
cooking, lifting handfuls of dough
and folding them into the muffin tins
or slipping her knife through the stems

of broccoli, they stood around
the kitchen and watched, got beers
from the refrigerator, pulled chairs
in from the dining room and sat like

men in a barbershop while she talked
and cooked. Hanno the sculptor walked up
behind her when she was knifing the lamb
to see if it was done. He had an opinion:

she should turn off the oven, put
the lamb back in, and it would be perfect.
He rubbed her shoulders with his
enormous hands. Bruce mentioned her

daughter, her novel. He seemed to know
about her past. The lamb reminded him
of Greece—Easter, the sea, how cheap
it used to be. Martha sat on the stainless

steel table while the pasta boiled,
the broccoli boiled, the rolls baked,
and the lamb rested in the oven.
Now, at the party, she wants to dance.

Cheerful, easy, she invites them
to dance, any of them, the seven artists
in the studio, young men from New York,
Washington, Idaho. They who were at home

in her kitchen now seem awkward,
hesitant. She stands in front of them,
dancing already. Motown from the boom
box moves up her body. Her feet twist

on the concrete like brushes on the drums.
Knees, breasts, everything is connected
yet going its own way. Her arm rises
over her head as though she were cracking

a blacksnake whip, gently, with pleasure.
One by one, they join her, making the right
motions with their feet, their hips, while Martha
dances, the juice of the music pulsing,

her face at ease, coming close to theirs,
daring them. They are bigger than she is,
especially Hanno the sculptor, who holds her
close to him, dancing in the old-fashioned way,

until she spins loose and vibrates in the flow
of music like a fish holding its place
in the rush of white water. Why are they
uneasy, backing away a little? They know her,

they've talked in the kitchen while she cleaves
chicken at the joints. They are at home
with women. But now, when her shoulders
and hips and knees hum to each other

over the long distance wires, the sculptors
strain against wood and stone, poets imagine
a Martha poem, not a description, not
a metaphor, not about her at all, but a poem

whose arms would rise in slow motion, one
then the other, cracking invisible whips.

Touch

On the plantation near Nairobi, Karen
Blixen's houseboy, Kamante, became
her chef—soups and sauces, fish in
white wine, artichokes. The Prince of
Wales praised his Cumberland Sauce.
Yet he never ate these dishes. "He did
at times taste the food that he cooked,
but then with a distrustful face, like a
witch who takes a sip out of her caul-
dron."

—*Out of Africa*

He has a *touch*. Does that imply
love for the thing created?
A trader masters the sleights

and feints of the futures market
but feels, himself, no greed,
no desire for anything

another million might buy.
A lover, having perfected
all the moves, uses his own

indifference to assure
his mastery of the craft.
Or a portrait painter, knifing in

the subtle shades of character,
feels an ashy gray
contempt for both his subjects

and their images.
The third-year child arranges
syllables in patterns

intricate as light
on water—it's the uttering
itself she wants,

the colors daubed
on glass, flashing back
the world in their own

reckless gesturing.
An oboeist eases into a phrase,
lifts it, lingers over it,

passes it to the French horn,
then takes it back,
elaborates some minor

ornament, holds, hesitates,
and lets it fall.
He's Kamante in the kitchen.

Let the foreigners reach deep
into the pot for essences
that may be blending there,

let them define the way the thyme
and coriander cling
along the margins of the palate.

He stirs over the wood fire,
watches the slow bubbles
swell and break.

Lullaby after the Rain

It rained all day today.
Now, under the moon's
half-open eye, the mole
noses his way

through the damp loam
under the roots
where the fat grubs sleep.
He's home,

earth muscling
around him wet and warm.
Grubs, say his blind eyes,
grubs and *spring.*

A snail slides through grass,
antennae pulling in
the news—the massacres
and meannesses

that people sleep with—
takes it in, digests it,
lays it in a thin
silver path

across the walk. Small
repairs, a cottage industry.
Moon eases west and down.
Some petals fall.

Night Song

Night waves curl in
over the rocks, then sigh
back to the sea.

Their muttering
has put the gulls to sleep,
and up on the slope

cows drop to their elbows
and sink into grass.
All creatures sleep,

except the fish.
We'd like to think
that fingerlings lie

on their side,
drifting, asleep
in the swing of salt

water, and halibut
snooze belly-up
in the silt. But no,

all night long,
barracuda weave and angle
through the weeds,

bluefins rise, flash
in the broken moonlight,
and dive again.

Sharks graze old wrecks
and marlins
slice the dark.

Responsibility

. . . and make our lives the theater
for many strange delights
for which we'll twist and shout
and sometimes even sing,
as if we didn't know the meaning
of the word *responsibility*. . . .
                    —*Tony Hoagland*

I came upon Tony's poem and spring
the same day. The hundred-year-old
cherry wept a waterfall of bloom,

which somehow turned to mist
before it hit the ground. These two—
the poem and spring—felt

like Jesus saying "Let it go,"
and sure enough I did it, I gave up,
I let the season ease me

out of myself. My friends became
a circle of the saints cheering
the spirit that spoke in tongues

out of my mouth. I grinned, I slept,
I ate a second helping of the loaves
and fishes. Now, I pass a woman

in the window of an all-night
restaurant. She smiles, only a little
surprised to see me there, and motions

me in. Her talk is effortless,
rephrasing the most poignant times.
I'm not staying. It's a new life now,

new pleasures—joy, in fact.
But that woman has nothing in the world
to do but put herself where I will come

upon her—her reckless eye, an elbow
drawn across a breast, a foot flamingo-like
against her knee. How easy to go back

to her, the slippery step-by-step
descent into responsibility. How sensuous
her breath, her hands. I comb her long

dark hair, braiding and rebraiding it.

C r i c k e t s

Insistent, you said—but no,
they don't insist. There's nothing
demanded or hinted at, no moral
in the small surge of their singing,
their scrapes and whistles.

Here, in a valley that angles up
from the coast, I like to count
the world's slow pulse, a wave breaking
on the beach below, then the sob
of surf withdrawing, until
another great crest foams and crashes.
But tonight the water's calm.
The moon spreads its clear lacquer
over the ocean and the slope
of land. A train groans north,
its heavy beat bending
the rails, *boxcar, boxcar,*
boxcar, and then the caboose
clearing the air. Leaving crickets.

Maybe they do insist,
as the night smell of a meadow
insists, an urging left over
from cows and rain and windfall pears
rotting back to seeds.

You're far inland tonight. I like
to think that words might carry
not through the upper air
but low along the rocks and droppings
of this pasture, over foothills

and a ridge of mountains, moved
by a hoarse rhythm, an undervoice
between us. It won't be long.
I'll find you in a room with windows
open to the surf of crickets, insistent
as the hollows of the sea.

An Anniversary

This is a dress
made of forty
ragged words we've
sewn together
haphazardly. Yes,
it fits, but now
it's time to rip
the seams, undo
the syllables one
by one until you
are naked again
in my hands.

*T*hree

On the Promontory

All things are an exchange for fire.
　　　　　　　—Heraclitus

You can believe it on a day like this
when haze hangs on the islands and the sea
smolders against the sky. Here on the headlands,

the long blue swells ease in from the Aegean,
leisurely as childhood, then churn and swirl
on these volcanic rocks, blaze up

in a white flame, and fall, becoming ash
and undertow. Here at the joint of youth
and age, spume flares, and all

this blue, the breath of a woman rising
and falling in sleep, all this is fire.

Descartes: A Lecture at the Sea

We still can stand on the headlands
looking down, as when Descartes,
having doubted everything,
came to a lovely certainty,
the motions of his mind distinct
and clear as water forming, churning,
reforming in sunlight, the patterned
swirls the one sure thing among
the doubtful rocks. And yet the world
crept back. *God, if he exists,*
enjoys every perfection; existence
is one perfection; therefore God
exists—a God whose truth could not
deceive our senses. This line
of reasoning restored it all:
the eye's impressions, the confused
news of hunger, thirst, and pain,
the gray gulls hanging like wrong ideas
on a shifty wind. Descartes, who knew
his essence was a simple, bodiless
thing, must have wept to see the *cogito*
give way to this sad mingling, the breaking
of pure pattern on the shore.

O m e n s

In Apollo's shrine at Sura, sacred fish
in a tank foretold the future as they schooled
or scattered, circled or flashed off to the right.

The fountain at Daphne murmured prophecies.
The priestess of Apollo at Epirus
tended a pit of serpents in the holy

grove, predicting harvests, good or bad,
as the snakes came to her willingly
or not. And now a falcon dropping on

a prairie dog portends the fall of some
fat dynasty. The sky cracks open. I
myself can see the future in a flash

of earrings clear across a room. With omens
everywhere, how did I wait till now
to turn my hand and check the palm—this hand

that I have carried at arm's length for all
these years. There was the future all along
where the deep lines converge under the thumb,

where the curled fingers dig in. Gently you open
my hand on top of your own thin palm. Yes,
read it to me, running your nail down

the old grooves, the silences, the looping
telephone lines. Why didn't I open my hand
to you back when the future was still a guess,

a premonition, a thin hope wavering
across the flesh? Look. That spidery spot
far to the right—wouldn't you say

the lines are still unsettled, snakes
just now uncoiling, making up their minds?
Wouldn't you say a choice could still be made?

Heraclitus on Fire

Thales thought the world was water.
Anaximenes said air—
or rather *aer,* which is to say
a mist or vapor. On any late
spring morning in Miletus, there
it is, *aer,* hovering where the road
dips toward the sea. If you sit
for an hour, on a rock, you almost
see its double metamorphosis:
easing upward as the day rises,
becoming air and fire,
and drawing itself together on
the petal of a columbine
and sliding, water now, down
the thin stem to take the shape
of earth. *Aer* it is, by observation
and sweet symmetry, the central stuff
to which all this returns.

But Heraclitus knows the *one*
is fire, the insubstantial blaze
that changes everything. Pythagoras,
Xenophanes, and Hesiod
knew many things but failed
to understand, refused to see
the forest leaping to become
the red it really is beneath
the apparent green, refused to feel
in their own flesh the unexpected
kindling and the going out.

Meeting, at a Party, a Woman with an Artificial Larynx

"How do you do," she says, her lips and tongue
shaping the words but the voice flat, metallic,
a wire on which the other voices hang
like laundry flapping. I think I hear a click
where a thought ends. She speaks of her fear
of the disease, how her real sadness
is her brother's suicide a year
ago—compared with others, how lucky she is
with husband and son. Her eyes and hands rise,
but that bare voice, emotionless and taut!

This woman draws words up from underground
where each syllable has hardened
for a hundred years, making her steel voice
an oracle—not riddling, but sounding a pitch
as plain as rails that narrow into sky.
The voice speaks bare events, over which
the elaborations of our talk
somersault and twist and fall and break.

Begonias

Snow settles on the begonias
blooming ragged
by the side door, leaves
and flowers whited out,
erased. Now or never—
so he snips
the long stems, dozens of them,
shakes off the snow,
and carries them
to the kitchen table.
Every vessel sprouts
begonias. He pays the bills,
tries to read, but
his eye drifts to the jointed
stems zigzagging out
of the water, the leaves
light green, dark green,
and bronze, and the flowers
rising or keeling over
with a spray of yellow stamens.
Three stems in a vase
compose themselves
without him. Whichever
way they angle
and twist, it seems right,
perfect.
There should be some
Japanese category for each
arrangement—*lame stork
in reeds* or *girl with hair
over eyes*. Even the gone
flowers, shrinking back
to seed, curl in
to the cupped hand
of a leaf.

Father Alfaro

The venerable ascetic, Luis Neri de Alfaro, Oratory priest, builder of the church at Atotonilco, Mexico

His meals were always meager, barely enough to stave off hunger. When he found some morsel to be to his liking, he would leave off eating immediately, or would nonchalantly, so as not to be noticed, mix into it some bitter aloe that he carried in his pocket. . . . The skeleton that you see at the foot of that pyre was his inseparable bedmate for many years, and he had it near his bed until the day before his death, when I ordered that it be taken away without his noticing.

*—Doctor Gamarra in his eulogy for
Father Alfaro*

Some pleasures may be harmless, Father.
The avocado ready to drop from the tree
behind the chapel—would it be tempting gluttony
to lift the crusty skin, slice green
and yellow wedges, sprinkle on salt,
and let God's plenty melt around the teeth?

Perhaps not, Alfaro replies.

And the hot springs, there through the grove of cedars,
where the Chichimecas come to ease the flesh,
to sing, even, and dance—a place, you say,
"of lawlessness and sensuality."
Setting aside the appetites you saw
fermenting there, let's consider the springs,
coppery water oozing up into
a shallow pool, hot water on the skin
after a hard day planting squash and clearing
irrigation ditches. Cool wind comes up
at evening, and the people slip
into the churning heat, lean their heads
against a stone, and soak away the world—
at least one day's aches and hungers.

What do you think, Alfaro?
Should they turn down this gift?

You answer your own question, calling it
a gift. What else?

Well, you speak of "music, feasts, and other
sins." Those reedy pipes the Chichimecas
finger on the streets—eerie intervals
like the thin whistle of the kiskadee
or else an abandoned soul calling out
from the mouth of an empty jar. Doesn't feeling
pour in through the ear?

It does. It does. But your metaphors—
have you considered where they'll lead?

That earthen jar leads me to a scene
your disciple Pocasangre painted there
beside the altar in the chapel—Virtues
and Vices, young Patience, for example, smiling
gently while a brute raises a stick
to bash him on the head. Would it be
retrograde to love the curving blue
and rust and gold, the robes, the jugs and fruit,
the faces round and placid in among
the torments? That humped-up monkey riding Judas'
back—all those arching lines, that life,
you must be drawn to it. Atotonilco's
dusky walls are glazed with it, as though
young Pocosangre, who meant to paint in smoke,
reached out and filled his brush with sky and grasses
by mistake. You must be drawn to it!

Certainly I'm drawn. On my best days
it's the meanings there that draw me.

But where are the meanings? Patterns
of light, the infinite articulations
of the voice and wind, what the tongue
intuits or what the body's always known—
doesn't meaning uncurl from the lime
and fiber of this soil? Doesn't it
split a seed and put out leaves, drenching
the air, sometimes, with the most improbable
blooms? This soil. What else is there?

You see. It's all been
leading to that question.

Love Poem with Scenery

Our friends are dying—Kitty Steele,
Don Kinsman—while we mourn here
on the roof, wrapping sun and wind

around our necks like a long scarf
woven there to the west
in Guanajuato. They die—

still funny, quick, generous,
no tapering off, just dead.
At first, everything seems absolute,

the bells, the long-armed spiky cactus,
its red flowers clustered in eights,
the splash all afternoon of our neighbor's

pretentious fountain, two narrow
cypresses twisting and weaving
beyond the clump of green

they call *trueno*. But further out
beyond the dammed-up lake,
sight blurs to haze,

a blowing dune of mountain,
and then another rise
that might just be

the sky. They're dead.
And that's us, gone any minute now
to some bright dust out there.

What will be left? Daughters,
students, friends—and a long love,
a love so steady I almost forget

I walk in it all day
like air, like the down-winding call
of the canyon wren, like the faint smell swung

from some censer far upwind, blessing me
with woodsmoke. To think that I,
awkward, unhandsome, should have been

loved, just matter-of-factly loved
with no subjunctives, no riffling
through old possibilities.

We knew each other a few months
and were married, ignorant
and lucky. I was baffled,

gradually getting the hang of this
new tongue in which you were
so fluent. You've always had a gift—

tutoring foreigners desperate to speak.
Gradually, I slurred my way
to new inflections, rolled *r*'s,

idioms that can't quite be translated.
And now, after daughters, deaths,
lives lost and found, love eases back

toward silence—or no, not silence
but a half-speech that slips
into the curve of back

and belly, spooned together
under the blankets, calling each other
out of bad dreams,

as, here on the roof, sun and wind
move through each other's body.
Gusts. Streams of vapor torn

from the full, white cloud.
Then the air calms.
Clothes on the neighbor's line

relax, dangle their knees
in a shoeless shuffle.
Red globs of *noche buena* sway

against a whitewashed wall.
I can call the names, *mesquite,*
espino, calasuche, but they stay

rooted on this dry plateau
until you bring the verbs,
white birds winging from dome to dome

across the blue. Or, look,
a wavery line of blackbirds, more
and more of them, measuring the rim

of some great broken bowl.
Birds slide over
into syllables, and syllables

translate to touch.
Wind and sun, which might have been
numbers on a chart, twist

in your hand, becoming
this quick light.

Shepherd

There was music in that barren place
already. While sheep grazed, the thin clank
of bells hung about them like a mist. Above,
we listened to that hollow clatter—no beat,

no tune, but a tinny music sweet as crickets.
And of course we knew the stars. At night
we'd find a rock that had stored up some warmth,
lean back, and name the sky as it crept west.

But the star that night—a fleck of white fire
low in the east, an open eye. And music
like voices calling, sinking in crevasses
behind us, and calling again. No wind

could make that sound, and there was no wind.
We set out in a sort of trance. And found . . .
what? An ordinary child, I guess—
a lamb bleary with birth. But music still hung

on the air like the sharp smell of sage
at the first of spring. We stood silent awhile,
then climbed back to our rocky ledge,
lay in the cold and watched the ancient shapes

circling: the serpent and the scorpion,
the bear sniffing around the pole, the fish,
the greater and the lesser dog, the ram—
and the milky road across the dark.

Staring, I thought I saw that road become
numberless egrets flying south, or sheep
with no one herding them, millions of sheep
moving beyond the borders of the night.

El Niño

Infant in the straw, breathing
with ox and ass under a clear sky—
this is the weather-child
we worship, Jesus, lord
of the ordinary. Send the winds
our houses are acquainted with,
drought in the dry season,
black clouds that churn
and rumble just when the final thirst
clutches our lips and throat.
This is the miracle we kneel to:
death when it's time for death.

Now, instead of the December
birth we know should come
on the longest night,
this vagrant Child, this Niño,
lurches, cries,
calls out from the salt spume.

We are children,
standing where our parents left us,
lonely, on a narrow rock,
watching the long surf
crash and rise.
Suddenly, you, Child, hold out
your arms, those hooks
and swirls, curled eyes
gathering out of deepest green.
You draw us
to your enormous heart,
lift us, sweep us downwind,
terrified, cradled
in a breaking wave.

The Spit

Offshore, below this spit
of land, a woman wind-surfs, her knees
giving with the rise

and drift of water. She toes
the board into the wind, steps
across the bow, and comes

about—tacking the sea slopes,
a woman with the wind
in her pocket. Her shoulder

brushes the waves that lift and turn
her, but she concedes
nothing. She tucks the board

under the lip of a wave, riding
the steep water, twisting the surge
to her own uses.

Now she diminishes downwind,
making the distance seem
immense between herself

and the high ground,
this spit turning
over the blue-white flames.

The Slurry

I mean to walk in through this emptiness.
When indolence has thinned me down
to a blue haze on water, when my voice

fades to the faint reverberation of
a bell on a lost goat's neck in another
country, then I may overhear the random

shifts and mutterings of the unseen world.
Now, delicately, now, with the fragile opposite
of will, I slip into the unformed slurry,

salt to the reckless sea, where all there is
is change, the swirl and drift of everything
that has evaded thought. Sorrow detached

from. So. Longing all the way in.
A squirming of fishes. Flounder and fall.
Insinuations under the scales, thin arms

that wave and disappear. The whirlpool.
The whirlpool. Lights out, she said, this is blood
Sunday, salt and salt. And you my daughters,

sweet eels, slippery. Tough muscle. What word
garbles the dark, tossing and turning? What sleep?
But even sleep cannot undream the shape

of things. The eye, the surface-loving eye:
it sets the waves, calls back the sweep of clouds,
the cliff, the small, determined flame of poppies.